Astronomy Now!™

A Look at
EARTH

Mary R. Dunn

PowerKiDS
press™

New York

Dedicated to my dear friends, Beth and Camille

Published in 2008 by The Rosen Publishing Group, Inc.
29 East 21st Street, New York, NY 10010

First Edition

Editor: Amelie von Zumbusch
Book Design: Greg Tucker
Photo Researcher: Nicole Pristash

Photo Credits: Cover, pp. 7 (inset), 13 (main), 19 by Photodisc; pp. 5, 9, 11 (inset), 15, 17 (main), 17 (inset) © Shutterstock.com; p. 7 (main) by Digital Vision; p. 11 (main) © istockphoto.com/Ondrej Cech; pp. 12, 13 (lower), 13 (middle), 13 (top) © Getty Images; p. 21 by Harrison H. Schmitt/NASA.

Library of Congress Cataloging-in-Publication Data

Dunn, Mary R.
  A look at Earth / Mary R. Dunn. — 1st ed.
      p. cm. — (Astronomy now)
  Includes index.
  ISBN-13: 978-1-4042-3827-5 (lib. bdg.)
  ISBN-10: 1-4042-3827-1 (lib. bdg.)
  1. Earth—Juvenile literature. I. Title.
  QB631.4.D86 2008
  525—dc22
                                          2007003399

Manufactured in the United States of America

Contents

The Planet Earth

Earth is one of the eight planets in our **solar system**. However, Earth is different from the other planets. It is the only planet known to have life! Plants, animals, and people live on Earth.

Earth has living things because it is far enough from the Sun to not get too many of the Sun's rays. However, Earth is still close enough for the Sun to warm it and keep it from becoming a land of ice. Earth has the gases that plants, animals, and people need, too. It even has water, which all living things need to live and grow.

Earth is the only planet in our solar system where animals, like these zebras, can live. No other planet supplies the water animals drink or the air they breathe.

5

Orbiting the Sun

Earth is the solar system's third planet from the Sun. Earth travels around the Sun in an **oval** path, called an orbit. It takes Earth 365 days, or one year, to finish its 595-million-mile (958 million km) orbit around the Sun.

All planets circle the Sun in orbits. The closer a planet is to the Sun, the faster the planet moves in its orbit. Earth travels at a speed of almost 19 miles per second (31 km/s). Scientists believe Earth's speed keeps it in its orbit. If the planet did not keep moving, it would be pulled into the Sun!

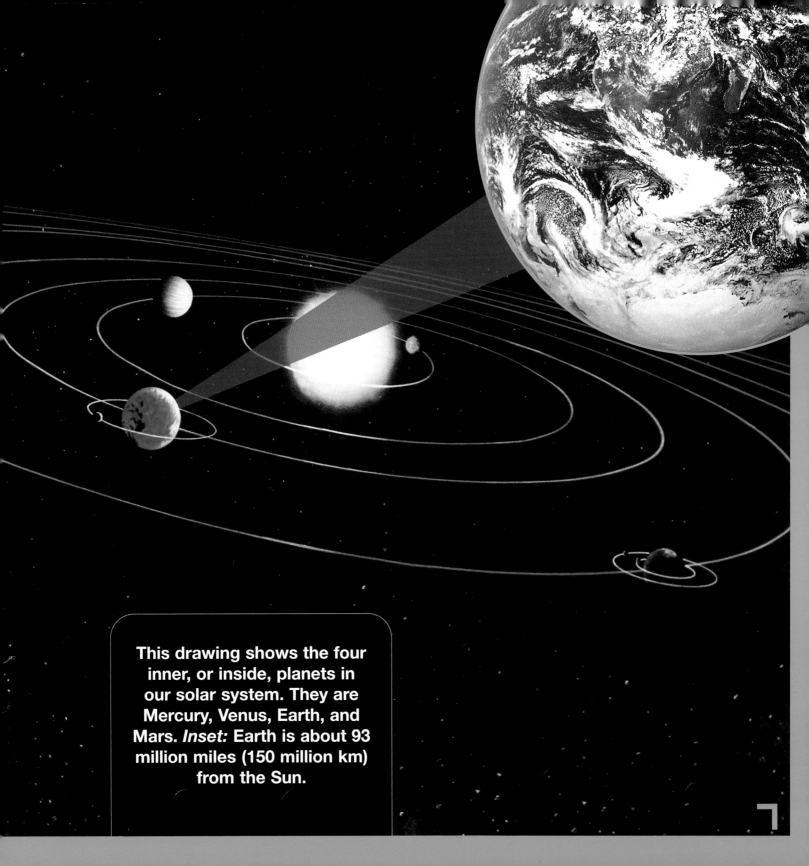

This drawing shows the four inner, or inside, planets in our solar system. They are Mercury, Venus, Earth, and Mars. *Inset:* Earth is about 93 million miles (150 million km) from the Sun.

Earth's Axis

Earth spins around an imaginary line through the middle of the planet. This line is called an axis. As Earth spins, one side of it faces the Sun. It is daytime on that side. The other side of Earth is in darkness, and it is nighttime. It takes Earth 24 hours to make one full turn on its axis.

Earth **tilts** on its axis. The part of Earth tilted toward the Sun gets more of the Sun's rays. This causes warmer weather. It is summer on that part of Earth. The part tilted away from the Sun has winter and colder weather.

It is daytime in Asia and eastern Africa in this picture of Earth. As Earth spins, it will become day in Europe and the rest of Africa and, later on, in North America and South America.

Earth's Atmosphere

At all times, Earth is covered by a blanket of air, called the **atmosphere**. The atmosphere keeps some of the Sun's unsafe rays from reaching Earth. It also keeps Earth safe from some of the **meteors** flying through space. The atmosphere burns most meteors up before they can crash into Earth.

Two important gases, nitrogen and oxygen, are in the lower part of the atmosphere. Nitrogen helps plants grow. Oxygen is a gas animals and people need to breathe in order to live. Earth's **gravity** holds the atmosphere close to the planet so that the gases will not move away.

Earth's atmosphere is many miles (km) thick and has several layers, or levels. *Inset:* The burning meteors that pass through Earth's atmosphere are also known as shooting stars.

11

Cool Facts

Earth is about 93 million miles (150 million km) from the Sun.

The first living things on Earth were in the oceans.

Earth is home to millions of different species, or kinds of living things. Thousands of new species are discovered each year.

Earth's Moon

Earth is the only planet with just one moon.

Because the Moon has no atmosphere, the footprints of the astronauts who have visited the Moon will stay there for millions of years.

By the year 2024, the United States hopes to build a Moon base where astronauts can live and work.

Footprint on the Moon

An Earth Timeline

1969 – Astronauts Neil Armstrong and Buzz Aldrin become the first people to walk on the Moon.

1959 – A spacecraft takes the first pictures of the side of the Moon that faces away from Earth.

1687 – Sir Isaac Newton explains how the Moon's gravity helps cause Earth's tides.

1543 – Nicolaus Copernicus figures out how to show that Earth moves around the Sun.

Earth's Oceans

Just as plants and animals need air, they also need water to live and grow. Earth is the one planet in our solar system that is mostly covered by water. In fact, nearly three-quarters of Earth is covered with water. Earth's water can be found in many bodies of water, such as rivers, lakes, and seas. The largest bodies of water are called oceans.

Oceans store heat in the warm seasons and give off heat in the cold seasons. This helps keep Earth's **temperature** just right for living things.

Earth's oceans are home to many forms of life. These include thousands of different kinds of fish and tiny animals called coral, which make up the bumpy, plantlike shapes seen here.

15

Inside Earth

Scientists study Earth's waters and atmosphere, but they also want to know what is deep inside Earth. To learn this, they study rocks that come out of **volcanoes**. They also have special tools to help them understand **earthquakes**.

Scientists have learned that a ball of hard iron and **nickel**, called the inner core, is at Earth's center. Hot, melted iron called magma covers the core and makes up the outer, or outside, core. Thick rock called the mantle lies past the magma. Rocks and dirt cover the mantle and make up Earth's crust. Plants, animals, and people all live on Earth's crust.

Crust

Mantle

Outer Core

Inner Core

Some volcanoes spill out only melted rock. Others, like the Karymsky Volcano, above, also shoot out ash and hard rocks. *Inset:* This cut-away drawing shows Earth's inner core, outer core, mantle, and crust.

The Moon

Some planets have many moons, but Earth has just one moon. You can see the Moon almost every night in the sky. Earth's Moon was formed over four **billion** years ago. The Moon is about one-quarter of the size of Earth. Scientists have learned that the Moon is cold and hard on the outside. They think its inside might be made of warm, melted matter.

Just as Earth orbits the Sun, the Moon orbits Earth. As it orbits Earth, the Moon's gravity pulls on Earth's axis. This pull helps cause tides in Earth's oceans.

The Moon has many bowl-shaped landforms called craters. These craters formed when rocks that were drifting through space crashed into the Moon.

Astronauts on the Moon

Since the 1960s, 12 **astronauts** have traveled to Earth's Moon. They dressed in special space suits to help them breathe and move around. The astronauts walked in the Moon's gray, dusty soil. They drove a small car called a lunar rover and visited rocky places called highlands. They found smooth **lava** flows called maria.

The astronauts brought more than 800 pounds (363 kg) of Moon rock and soil back to Earth. Scientists tested the rocks and proved there has never been water on the Moon. However, they found that, if they were watered, plants could grow in the Moon's soil.

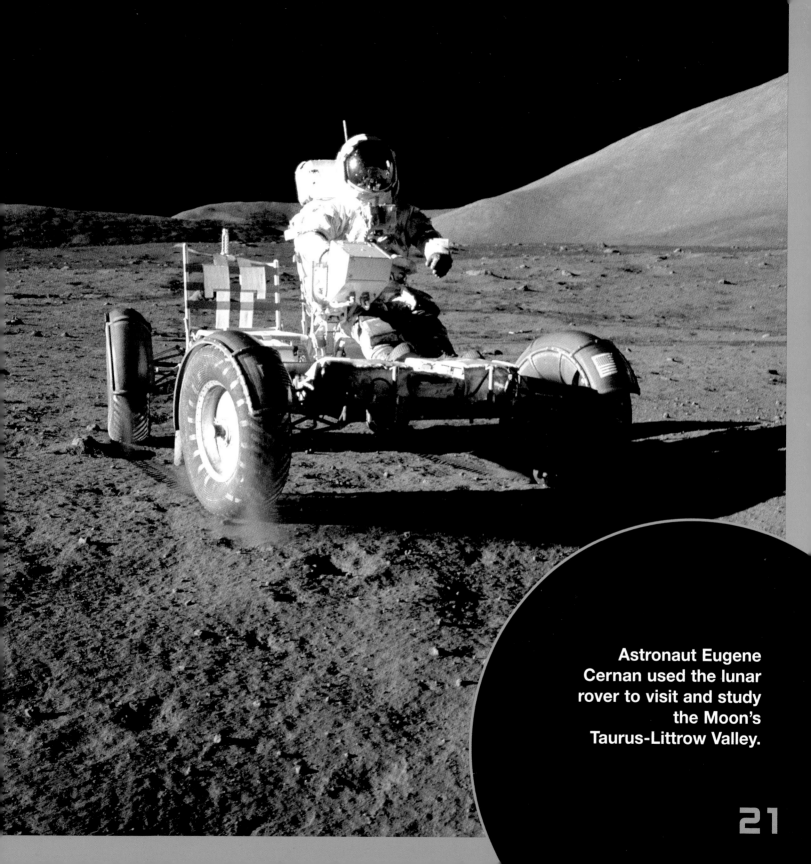

Astronaut Eugene Cernan used the lunar rover to visit and study the Moon's Taurus-Littrow Valley.

21

A Changing Planet

At the same time that they are learning about the Moon, scientists are studying our own Earth. Earth is always changing. Every day, pieces of Earth's crust move a tiny bit. Sometimes, the pieces move quickly and cause earthquakes. Earthquakes break down landforms. Floods wash away landforms. Volcanoes spill out lava and make new land.

People change Earth, too. We dam rivers, reshape beaches, and flatten land. Some of the changes people make hurt Earth. For example, some machines we use make gases that destroy Earth's atmosphere. All people should take good care of Earth, though. It is our home.

Glossary

astronauts (AS-truh-nots) People who are trained to travel in outer space.

atmosphere (AT-muh-sfeer) The gases around an object in space.

billion (BIL-yun) A thousand millions.

earthquakes (URTH-kwayks) Shakings of Earth's outside caused by the movement of large pieces of land called plates that run into each other.

gravity (GRA-vih-tee) The force that causes objects to move toward each other. The bigger an object is, the more gravity it has.

lava (LAH-vuh) Hot, melted rock that comes out of a volcano.

meteors (MEE-tee-orz) Rocks from outer space.

nickel (NIH-kel) A kind of hard, strong, silver-colored matter.

oval (OH-vul) A shape that looks like a circle with two sides pressed in.

solar system (SOH-ler SIS-tem) A group of planets that circles a star.

temperature (TEM-pur-cher) How hot or cold something is.

tilts (TILTS) Tips to one side.

volcanoes (vol-KAY-nohz) Openings in Earth that sometimes shoot up hot, melted rock called lava.

Index

A
animals, 4, 10, 14, 16
astronauts, 20
atmosphere, 10, 16, 22
axis, 8, 18

E
earthquakes, 16, 22

G
gas(es), 4, 10
gravity, 10, 18

I
ice, 4

L
life, 4

M
maria, 20
meteors, 10
Moon, 18, 20, 22

N
nickel, 16

P
people, 4, 10, 16, 22
plants, 4, 10, 14, 16, 20

S
scientists, 6, 16, 18, 20, 22
solar system, 4, 14
Sun, 4, 6, 8, 18

V
volcanoes, 16, 22

W
water(s), 4, 14, 16, 20

Y
year(s), 6, 18

Web Sites

Due to the changing nature of Internet links, PowerKids Press has developed an online list of Web sites related to the subject of this book. This site is updated regularly. Please use this link to access the list:
www.powerkidslinks.com/astro/earth/